DIANA

ROMAN GODDESS OF THE HUNT

by Amie Jane Leavitt

Content Consultant
Robyn Le Blanc, PhD
Assistant Professor of Classical Studies
University of North Carolina, Greensboro
Greensboro, NC

CAPSTONE PRESS
a capstone imprint

Snap Books are published by Capstone Press,
1710 Roe Crest Drive, North Mankato, Minnesota 56003
www.capstonepub.com

Library of Congress Cataloging-in-Publication Data
Names: Leavitt, Amie Jane, author.
Title: Diana : Roman goddess of the hunt / by Amie Jane Leavitt.
Description: 1st Ed. | North Mankato, MN : Capstone, 2019. | Series: Snap books.
Legendary goddesses Identifiers: LCCN 2019004855| ISBN 9781543574128
(hardcover) | ISBN 9781543575521 (pbk.) | ISBN 9781543574166 (eBook PDF)
Subjects: LCSH: Diana (Roman deity)—Juvenile literature. | Artemis
(Greek deity)—Juvenile literature. | Goddesses, Roman—Juvenile literature. |
Goddesses, Greek—Juvenile literature.
Classification: LCC BL820.D5 L43 2019 | DDC 292.2/114—dc23
LC record available at https://lccn.loc.gov/2019004855

Editorial Credits
Michelle Parkin, editor
Bobbie Nuytten, designer
Svetlana Zhurkin, media researcher
Katy LaVigne, production specialist

Image Credits
Alamy: Album, 15 (top); Bridgeman Images: Wonderwoman, 28; Dreamstime:
Joserpizarro, 18; Getty Images: Corbis/Stefano Bianchetti, 27; Newscom: akg-
images, 5, 24–25, Album/DC Entertainment/Warner Bros., 29 (right), United
Archives/Impress, 29 (left), Universal Images Group/De Agostini/W. Buss, 22;
Shutterstock: Brenda Kean, 7, Dotted Yeti, 10 (top), Evdoha_spb, cover, Gimas,
23, Masterrr, 16, 17, Oigres8, 26, Santia, 14, Vladimir Wrangel, 15 (bottom);
Wikimedia Commons: Daderot, 21, James Steakley, 19

Illustrations by Alessandra Fusi
Design Elements by Shutterstock

All internet sites appearing in back matter were available and accurate
when this book was sent to press.

Printed and bound in the USA.
PA70

TABLE OF CONTENTS

Chapter 1

DIANA MAKES ACTAEON PAY

Actaeon was one of the best hunters in the land. He spent much of his time deep in the forest, hunting deer with his friends and many dogs. Today was no different. The hunt had been long, and Actaeon was tired and thirsty. He and his friends decided to return to camp.

"Let's rest by the fire and enjoy a hearty meal," Actaeon suggested.

As the group made their way back to camp, Actaeon thought he heard the sound of splashing water in the distance.

Perhaps a stream or waterfall is nearby, Actaeon thought. *My throat is so dry. I'll stop for a drink.*

Separating from the group, Actaeon pushed through the dense trees. As he followed the sound of water, he heard something else. It was laughter. For a moment, Actaeon thought he should turn around. He didn't want to bother anyone up ahead. But he was thirsty. Surely a quick drink wouldn't hurt.

As Actaeon crept closer, he found the source of the laughter. A group of women were bathing in a sparkling spring. Actaeon stood in front of them, dumbfounded. When the women saw Actaeon standing there, they screamed and dove into the bushes.

"We are bathing in this water," they cried. "You cannot be here!"

"I am so sorry," Actaeon cried out, embarrassed. "I will leave right away."

But it was already too late for Actaeon. One of the bathing women was Diana, the Roman goddess of the hunt. She was not happy that Actaeon had invaded her privacy. In fact, she was furious.

"You will pay dearly for your prying eyes!" the goddess said angrily. And with that, she splashed Actaeon with water from the spring.

Actaeon turned and ran into the forest as fast as his legs could carry him. Suddenly, he felt his legs moving much faster than ever before. And it wasn't just his legs. His arms were now sprinting on the ground too.

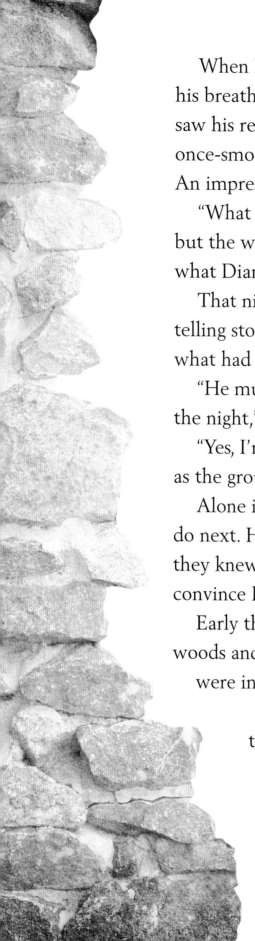

When he was out of danger, Actaeon paused to catch his breath near a small pool of water. But when he saw his reflection, he couldn't believe his eyes. His once-smooth skin was now covered in scratchy, gray fur. An impressive set of antlers grew from his head.

"What has happened to me?" Actaeon tried to shout, but the words would not come out. Actaeon realized what Diana had done. She had turned him into a deer!

That night Actaeon's friends relaxed around the fire, telling stories and eating a hearty meal. They wondered what had happened to him.

"He must have decided to camp somewhere else for the night," said one man.

"Yes, I'm sure he'll join us by morning," said another, as the group went to bed.

Alone in the woods, Actaeon thought about what to do next. He had to get a message to the other men. If they knew what happened to him, perhaps they could convince Diana to remove the spell.

Early the next morning, Actaeon strode through the woods and approached the camp. When his friends were in sight, he yelled out.

"Friends! It is I, Actaeon," he called. But all the men heard was a deep, husky bellow. They stood up and turned in Actaeon's direction.

"Look at that beautiful deer!" one man shouted.

"Let the dogs loose!" said another.

6

Actaeon saw the dogs running toward him. He burst out of the camp and into the forest. Actaeon galloped as fast as his four legs would carry him, but it didn't matter. The dogs were right on his heels. Eventually, they overtook him.

That night Actaeon's friends gathered again around the fire, telling stories and eating a hearty meal.

"Actaeon missed a great hunt today," one of his friends said. They all agreed. "He's always wanted to get a giant deer. I can't wait to tell him about it!"

consequence—the result of a person's actions

GODDESS FACT

The story of Diana and Actaeon shows that choices and behaviors have **consequences**. And most importantly, it taught the ancient people that angering the gods was dangerous.

Meaningful Myths

The ancient Romans told stories of gods and goddesses for many reasons. Some myths explained why things happened, such as disease, death, and the passing of time. Others were used to pass on oral traditions and keep the history of the ancient people alive. Still others were used to teach people the difference between right and wrong.

Chapter 2

THE BIRTH OF A GODDESS

In Roman **mythology**, gods and goddesses were **immortal** beings. Jupiter was the king of the Roman **deities**. His wife, Juno, was the goddess of marriage and the protector of the nation. The ancient Romans **worshipped** these gods in one of the most famous temples in Rome—the Capitoline Temple on the Capitoline Hill.

Just like the Greek deities, Roman gods and goddesses had many children together. Diana was the daughter of Jupiter and Latona, the goddess of motherhood. When Juno found out that Latona was pregnant with Jupiter's child, she was furious. As punishment, Juno banished Latona from the kingdom of the gods. But that wasn't enough. Latona wasn't allowed to have her child anywhere on Earth.

Latona desperately searched for a place to have her child. Eventually, Latona discovered a beautiful island called Delos. The island hovered just above the land. It was perfect. Latona climbed onto the soft, green island.

mythology—a collection of old or ancient stories told again and again

immortal—able to live forever

deity—a god or goddess

worship—to express love and devotion to a god

Even though Diana is the goddess of children, she was never a baby. Diana was born as a young woman, between the ages of 12 and 19.

After Diana was born, Latona continued to feel pain. Latona didn't know it but she was pregnant with twins! Diana helped her mother give birth to her brother Apollo. Because of this, Diana was known as a protector of women and the goddess of children and childbirth.

ANCIENT ORIGINS

The ancient Romans worshipped gods and goddesses from Greek mythology. But the Romans changed the deities's names. In Greek mythology, Diana was known as the goddess Artemis. Her mother Latona was called Leto. Diana's twin brother Apollo was one of the few gods who had the same name in Greek and Roman mythology.

·····GODDESS FACT·····

Most of the planets in our **solar system** were named after Greek and Roman gods. Earth is the only planet that wasn't.

Jupiter

ROMAN AND GREEK GODS

ROMAN NAME	GREEK NAME	ROLE
DIANA	ARTEMIS	goddess of the hunt, the woods, children, childbirth, the moon, and wild animals; protector of women
JUPITER	ZEUS	king of the gods
LATONA	LETO	goddess of motherhood
APOLLO	APOLLO	god of music and medicine; god of the sun, prophecy, and disease
JUNO	HERA	goddess of marriage
MINERVA	ATHENA	goddess of wisdom, war, and weaving
VESTA	HESTIA	goddess of home and family
NEPTUNE	POSEIDON	god of the sea
VENUS	APHRODITE	goddess of love
PLUTO	HADES	god of the **underworld**; god of wealth
CERES	DEMETER	goddess of the harvest
MARS	ARES	god of war
MERCURY	HERMES	messenger of the gods; god of travelers and merchants
CUPID	EROS	god of love

solar system—the sun and all the planets, moons, comets, and smaller bodies orbiting it

underworld—the place where ancient Romans believed spirits of the dead go

Chapter 3

THE MAIDEN GODDESS

Diana is considered a **maiden** goddess. She chose to never marry or have children. She was one of three maiden goddesses in Roman mythology. The other two were Minerva and Vesta.

CLOSE FRIENDSHIPS

Diana was friendly with spirits of the forests, woods, and plains. Her two closest friends were Egeria and Virbius. Egeria was a water **nymph**. She and Diana worked together to protect women during childbirth. Virbius was the god of the forests. Diana, Egeria, and Virbius made up a trinity of gods. They were sometimes worshipped together.

maiden—a young, unmarried woman

nymph—a mythical maiden on a mountain, in a forest, or in a body or water

GODDESS FACT

Virbius was once a human named Hippolytus, a loyal follower of Diana. When he died, Diana turned him into a god.

ORION

Diana was also friends with the giant, Orion. She would often hunt with him in the forests. But Apollo was jealous of Diana's friendship with the giant. Apollo tricked Diana into shooting Orion with an arrow during target practice. Orion was killed instantly. When she realized what she had done, Diana was devastated. She turned Orion into a **constellation** in the sky. Orion's constellation is still seen today.

constellation—a group of stars in the sky that seem to trace the outline of a person, animal, or object

Orion's Belt is made up of the three bright stars in the middle of the constellation.

Orion's Belt

14

The Story of Diana's Father

Diana comes from a long line of powerful Roman gods. Her father Jupiter was the king of the Roman gods. He was represented by light, thunder, and the sky. He was responsible for protecting the laws and people of ancient Rome.

Jupiter became king by overthrowing his father, Saturn. Years earlier, Saturn was warned that one of his children would take over his throne. Saturn had six children. After each child was born, Saturn swallowed the child. Saturn's wife, Ops, was desperate to save at least one of her children. When Jupiter was born, Ops wrapped a large stone in a blanket and handed it to Saturn. The god swallowed the stone, thinking it was his son. Jupiter was saved.

Years later Jupiter returned to battle his father for the throne and rescue his swallowed siblings. After a long war, Jupiter finally became king.

In a similar Greek myth, Zeus's mother Rhea gave a blanket-wrapped stone to her husband, Cronus. Like Saturn, he swallowed the stone instead of his son Zeus.

marble head of Jupiter

Diana's Family Tree

Diana's family consisted of her parents, Jupiter and Latona, and her twin brother Apollo. She also had many aunts, uncles, and half-siblings.

Diana's Uncles
PLUTO
NEPTUNE

Diana's Aunts
JUNO
VESTA
CERES

The Roman goddess of Earth was Diana's grandmother.

OPS

The king of the Roman gods was Diana's father.

JUPITER

The god of agriculture was Diana's grandfather.

SATURN

Diana's mother was the goddess of motherhood.

LATONA

······ grandparents
······ parents
······ aunts and uncles
······ siblings and half-siblings

Diana's Half-Siblings

VULCAN

VENUS

MINERVA

MERCURY

BACCHUS

MARS

PROSERPINA

DIANA

Diana's twin brother was the god of the sun.

APOLLO

Chapter 4

STRONG AND FEARLESS DIANA

In Roman myths, Diana often appeared as a young woman. She was tall, beautiful, and intelligent. She was often compared to Venus, one of the most beautiful goddesses in Roman mythology.

As the goddess of the hunt, Diana was a strong hunter. She could dart through forests and easily track wild animals. Diana wore a short buckskin **tunic**. The short dress helped her move quickly through the woods. Diana also wore hunting boots and a **crescent**-shaped crown on her head. Diana was also the goddess of the moon. In this role, she wore a long robe. A veil covered her head.

SYMBOLS AND ART

Diana carried a bow and a **quiver** of arrows. Her faithful hunting dog was by her side.

In works of art, Diana is shown as a young, beautiful huntress aiming her bow at a target. Because of her love of the forest, Diana is often painted near oak groves and cypress trees. A deer or she-bear is usually nearby. Sometimes Diana has wings and holds a deer, leopard, or lion. When depicted as the moon goddess, Diana sits on the moon or is hunting by moonlight.

tunic—a loose, sleeveless garment

crescent—a curved shape that looks like a moon when it is a sliver in the sky

quiver—a container for arrows

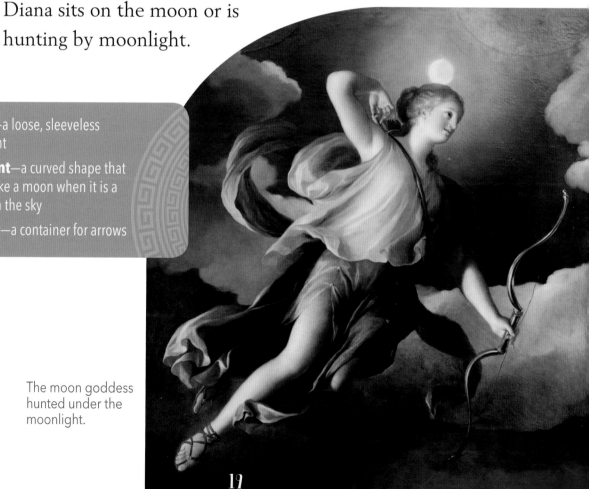

The moon goddess hunted under the moonlight.

SPECIAL POWERS

Diana had the power to talk to and control animals. She could also turn humans into animals, as she did with Actaeon. Diana helped women deliver healthy children. She took care of the newborn babies too. Diana kept them safe and protected them from illnesses.

····· GODDESS FACT ·····

A marble statue of Diana is at the Bode Museum in Berlin, Germany. It's called *Diana as Huntress*. Other famous statues include *Diana of Versailles* at the Louvre in Paris, France, and *Diana* in the Metropolitan Museum of Art in New York City.

Diana as Huntress

Chapter 5

WORSHIPPING DIANA

In ancient times, different groups of people worshipped Diana, including pregnant women and women who wanted children. Slaves and lower classes of people considered her a protector. As goddess of hunting and wild animals, people prayed for Diana's help to find food. People also believed she would protect them from wild animals in the forests.

Some Roman emperors worshipped Diana.

FOREST WORSHIP

People created **shrines** and temples to worship Diana. One of the first was near a small volcanic lake called Lake Nemi. This shrine was set in a grove of trees. People came there to worship Diana, Egeria, and Virbius.

It is believed that Virbius was Diana's first priest. But anyone else who wanted the job had to meet strict requirements. First, Diana's priest had to be a runaway slave. Second, he had to challenge the current priest to a duel. The challenger broke off a branch from one of Diana's sacred oak trees. Then he battled the current priest, who also fought with a sacred branch. The man who survived the fight became the new priest in Diana's temple.

shrine—a holy building that often contains sacred objects

23

SEVEN WONDERS OF THE WORLD

Another important place of worship was in Ephesus, an ancient city in Turkey. The Temple of Artemis was built there. Many times over several centuries, the temple was destroyed by either flooding or fire. Each time, it was rebuilt.

After the last fire, a new temple was built around 323 BC. It was made out of marble. The Roman writer Pliny said the temple was about 425 feet (129.5 meters) long and 225 feet (69 m) wide. He also said it took 120 years to complete!

When the temple was finished, it was considered one of the Seven Wonders of the Ancient World. It is mentioned several times in the New Testament of the Bible. In 268 AD, the temple was destroyed. Archaeologists discovered the temple's ruins in 1869.

the Temple of Artemis in Ephesus

FESTIVALS

Each year the ancient Romans held special festivals to honor Diana. They called them Nemoralia, or the Festival of the Torches. One was held at Diana's shrine near Lake Nemi. The other took place near her temple on Aventine Hill in Rome.

····· GODDESS FACT ·····

The Catholic Church adopted the Festival of the Torches, calling it the Feast of the Assumption of Mary. It is celebrated on August 15 every year in countries around the world.

The celebration began on August 13 and lasted for three days. On the first night, worshippers washed their hair and decorated it with flowers. Then they lit torches or candles and walked around Lake Nemi. The light would flicker off of the lake and reflect back like a sparkling mirror. During the festival, it was forbidden to hunt any forest animals.

Worshippers in Delos danced in a sacred forest to honor Diana.

GODDESS FACT

Today some religions still worship Diana on August 13.

DIANA IN POP CULTURE

The Roman goddess Diana has influenced pop culture today. DC's Wonder Woman is based on the Roman goddess. This includes her name, Diana Prince. The character has long, flowing dark hair and wears a crescent-shaped crown, a short tunic, and tall hunting boots. In DC's story, Wonder Woman protects the Amazons, a group of warrior women.

The character of Wonder Woman was introduced in 1941, in the All Star Comics #8. In the story, Wonder Woman is named Diana after her grandmother, who is the goddess of the moon.

Wonder Woman appeared on the cover of *Sensation Comics* in January 1942.

The comic book was turned into a TV series in 1975, with Lynda Carter starring as the superhero goddess. In 2017, the movie *Wonder Woman* introduced a new audience to Diana. The goddess was played by Gal Gadot.

Gal Gadot as Wonder Woman

Lynda Carter played Wonder Woman from 1975 until 1979.

GLOSSARY

consequence (KAHN-suh-kwens)—the result of a person's actions

constellation (kahn-stuh-LAY-shuhn)—a group of stars in the sky that seem to trace the outline of a person, animal, or object

crescent (KRE-suhnt)—a curved shape that looks like a moon when it is a sliver in the sky

deity (DEE-uh-tee)—a god or goddess

immortal (i-MOR-tuhl)—able to live forever

maiden (MAYD-uhn)—a young, unmarried woman

mythology (mi-THOL-uh-jee)—a collection of old or ancient stories told again and again

nymph (NIMF)—a mythical maiden on a mountain, in a forest, or in a body of water

quiver (KWIV-ur)—a container for arrows

shrine (SHRINE)—a holy building that often contains sacred objects

solar system (SOH-lurh SISS-tuhm)—the sun and all the planets, moons, comets, and smaller bodies orbiting it

tunic (TOO-nik)—a loose, sleeveless garment

underworld (UHN-dur-wurld)—the place where ancient Romans believed spirits of the dead go

worship (WUR-ship)—to express love and devotion to a god

READ MORE

Ganeri, Anita. *Star Stories: Constellation Tales from Around the World.* Philadelphia: Running Press Kids, 2019.

Korté, Steve. *Wonder Woman and the World of Myth.* Wonder Woman Mythology. North Mankato, MN: Capstone Press, 2017.

Temple, Teri, and Emily Temple. *Diana: Goddess of Hunting and Protector of Animals.* Roman Mythology. Mankato, MN: Childs World, 2015.

INTERNET SITES

Ducksters Education Site: Ancient Rome Gods and Mythology https://www.ducksters.com/history/ancient_roman_gods_mythology.php

National Geographic: The Gods and Goddesses of Ancient Rome https://www.nationalgeographic.org/news/gods-and-goddesses-ancient-rome/

INDEX